WAC JOKES

Also published by Corgi Books

WAC SNAX

WAC JOKES

GYLES BRANDRETH
with
TOMMY BOYD,

ARABELLA WARNER
and **JAMES BAKER**

**ILLUSTRATED BY
SCOULAR ANDERSON**

CORGI BOOKS

WIDE AWAKE CLUB: WAC JOKES
A CORGI BOOK 0 552 54279 2

First published in Great Britain by Corgi Books

PRINTING HISTORY
Corgi edition published 1986
Corgi edition reprinted 1987

Corgi Books are published by Transworld Publishers Ltd., 61–63 Uxbridge Road, Ealing, London W5 5SA, in Australia by Transworld Publishers (Aust.) Pty. Ltd., 15–23 Helles Avenue, Moorebank, NSW 2170, and in New Zealand by Transworld Publishers (N.Z.) Ltd., Cnr. Moselle and Waipareira avenues, Henderson, Auckland.

Printed and bound in Great Britain by
Cox & Wyman Ltd., Reading, Berks.

CONTENTS

WELCOME!

A WORD OF WARNING

This book is dangerous. Well, it had me in stitches. If you die laughing don't blame us. Blame the Wide Awake Club viewers because all the jokes came from them. They've sent us thousands and we've chosen the ones that hurt most!

Have fun!

Gyles Brandreth

WAC JOKE CORRESPONDENT

ANIMAL CRACKERS

*At WAC we love animals. We also love jokes. So when we come across animal jokes we go **WILD!***

What would you do if you discovered an elephant sleeping in your bed?
Sleep somewhere else.

What do geese watch on television?
Duckumentaries.

What do polar bears eat for lunch?
Iceburgers.

What did the farmer give his pig when he discovered it had a sore throat?
Oinkment.

What did the baby porcupine say when he backed into a cactus?
Is that you, Mum?

Why do mother kangaroos hate rainy weather?
Because their children have to play inside.

What is white, furry, and smells like a peppermint?
A polo bear.

Sally: Did you hear what happened to the jellyfish?
Nick: No, what happened?
Sally: It set.

What would you get if you crossed a skunk with a boomerang?
A nasty smell you can't get rid of.

What did the cowboy say when his dog fell over the cliff?
Dawg-gone!

What kind of tiles can you never stick on a wall?
Reptiles?

Why is a pig like a horse?
When a pig is hungry he eats like a horse, and when a horse is hungry he eats like a pig.

What is another name for a baby whale that cries all the time?
A little blubber.

What did the Spanish farmer say to his chickens?
Oh, lay!

What would you get if you crossed a set of bagpipes with a frog?
Hopscotch.

What animal do you look like when you get into the bath?
A little bear.

Why did the skunk take an aspirin?
To cure his stinking headache.

What did the Daddy goat say to the baby goat?
You can't kid me.

What has twelve legs, six ears and one eye?
Three blind mice and half a kipper.

Why wouldn't the little pigs listen to their
father?
Because he was such a boar.

Tommy: What kind of dog is *that*?
Timmy: A police dog!
Tommy: He doesn't look much like a police dog
to me!
Timmy: That's because he's a plain clothes
police dog!

What is a crocodile's favourite game?
Snap!

What goes 'Croak! Croak!' when it is misty?
A frog-horn.

What would you get if you crossed rabbits with
leeks?
Bunions.

Why does an elephant have a trunk?
**So he has somewhere to hide when he sees a
mouse.**

What name would you give to a cat who joins
the Red Cross?
A first-aid kit.

Did you hear what happened to the flea-circus?
A dog walked by and stole the show.

How do monkeys toast their bread in the jungle?
They put it under the griller.

What happens when ducks fly upside down?
They quack up.

What is worse than a giraffe with a sore throat?
A giraffe with a stiff neck.

What is the difference between an elephant and a flea?
An elephant can have fleas, but a flea cannot have elephants.

Which are the world's most mathematical animals?
Rabbits — because they multiply so well.

Why wouldn't the rooster fight?
Because he was a chicken.
What do Eskimos call their cows?
Eskimoos.

What is big, grey, and goes around muttering?
A Mumbo-Jumbo.

Gyles: I'm worried about my baby owl.
James: Why's that?
Gyles: Because he doesn't give a hoot about anything.

What happens when you put snakes on a car window?
You get windshield vipers.

What animal could you put in a washing
machine?
A wash-and-were-wolf.

Where do all good turkeys go when they die?
To oven.

How many fish can you put in an empty pond
that is 60cm square?
One — after that it is not empty.

Why did the lobster blush?
Because it saw the salad dressing.

What is black and white and red all over?
An embarrassed zebra.

What do you get if you cross a parrot with a
woodpecker?
**A bird that knocks on doors and delivers
messages.**

Arabella: Who has a parrot which shouts, 'Pieces of four! Pieces of four!'
Natasha: Short John Silver, of course!

Why do white sheep eat more than black sheep?
Because there are more of them.

What is an octopus?
An eight-sided cat.

Which animals did not go on to the ark in pairs?
Worms — they went in apples.

What did the stag say to his children?
Hurry up, deer.

Why is a rabbit's nose always shiny?
Because its powder puff is at the wrong end.

On which side does a chicken have most feathers?
On the outside.

What do you call a camel with three humps?
Humphrey.

What would you get if you crossed a hedgehog with a mole?
A tunnel that leaks.

What do you call a bald rabbit?
Hareless.

What is the best thing to give a seasick hippopotamus?
Plenty of room.

Who always goes to sleep with his shoes on?
A horse.

What part of a fish weighs the most?
The scales.

What can fly under water?
A fly in a submarine.

Sally: Have you ever seen a horse that could count?
James: No, but I've seen a spelling bee.

What do porcupines eat with their cheese?
Prickled onions.

What is the place called where you weigh whales?
A whale-weigh station.

Why did the moth chew a hole in the carpet?
Because it wanted to see the floor show.

WAC SNAX

WAC Snax are delicious recipes devised by wide-awake cooks across the country. Look out for the book of them published by Corgi. This chapter is good enough to eat — it is full of jokes with a foodie flavour.

Waiter: Would you like some idiot soup, Sir?
Customer: What's idiot soup?
Waiter: Thick soup.

How many peas in a pint?
Only one.

Customer: Waiter, waiter, why does this crab only have one claw?
Waiter: I'm sorry, Sir — it was in a fight.
Customer: Well, then, bring me the winner.

Customer: Waiter, waiter, there's a dead fly in my soup.
Waiter: Yes, Sir — it's the hot water that kills them.

What is green, leafy and goes around at 120 mph?
A lettuce Elan.

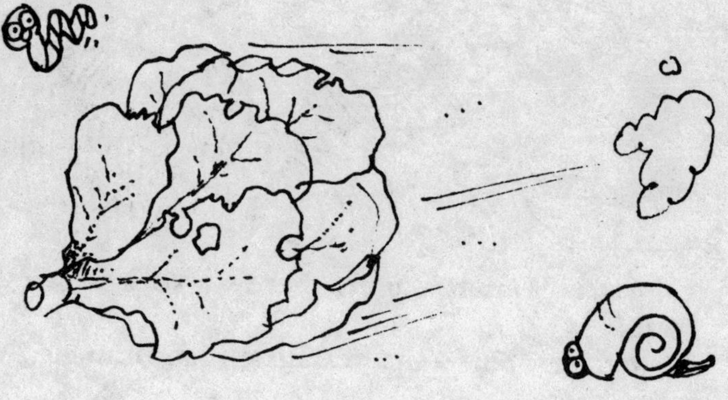

James: Did you hear about the two potatoes who didn't see eye to eye?
Nick: No, what happened?
James: When one took his jacket off, the other thought he'd had his chips.

Customer: Waiter, waiter, what do I have to do to get a glass of water in this place?
Waiter: Set yourself alight, Sir.

Customer: Waiter, waiter, there's a dead beetle in my wine.
Waiter: Well, Sir — you did ask for something with a little body in it.

Customer: Waiter, waiter, there's a stick in my soup.
Waiter: Yes, Sir — this restaurant has branches everywhere.

Customer: Waiter, waiter, are there any menus in this place?
Waiter: No, Sir.
Customer: Then how do I know what you have?
Waiter: Look at the table cloth and guess, Sir.

Customer: Waiter, waiter, you're not fit to serve a pig!
Waiter: I'm trying my best, Sir.

Customer: Waiter, waiter, this plate is damp.
Waiter: That's your soup, Sir.

Customer: Waiter, waiter, there's a button in my salad!
Waiter: Sorry, Sir — it must have fallen off when the salad was dressing.

What do geese eat?
Gooseberries.

Customer: Waiter, waiter, have you smoked salmon?
Waiter: No, but I once smoked a pipe.

Customer: Waiter, waiter, your thumb is in my soup!
Waiter: Don't worry, Sir — it's not hot.

Customer: Waiter, waiter, do you call this a three-course meal?
Waiter: Yes, Sir — two peas and a chip.

Customer: Waiter, waiter, there's no chicken in this chicken pie!
Waiter: No, Sir — and you won't find any shepherds in the shepherds pie, either.

Sally: Why did the baker stop making doughnuts?
Arabella: I don't know — why did the baker stop making doughnuts?
Sally: Because he got tired of the hole business.

Customer: Waiter, waiter, is this a lamb chop or a pork chop?
Waiter: Can't you tell the difference, Sir?
Customer: No, I can't.
Waiter: Then it doesn't matter, does it?

Customer: Waiter, waiter, I'd like a hamburger, please.
Waiter: With pleasure, Sir.
Customer: No, with relish and lots of onions, please.

Customer: Waiter, waiter, do you have frogs' legs?
Waiter: No, Sir — it's rheumatism that makes me walk like this.

Where do tough chickens come from?
Hard-boiled eggs.

Customer: Waiter, waiter, this soup is poisonous!
Waiter: Who told you that, Sir?
Customer: A little swallow.

Customer: Waiter, waiter, are the table cloths ever changed here?
Waiter: Don't ask me, Sir — I've only been working here a year.

Customer: Waiter, waiter, is this tea or coffee? It tastes like petrol.
Waiter: That's coffee, Sir — the tea tastes like paraffin.

Tommy: Why did the writer put his finger in the alphabet soup?
Gyles: I don't know — why did the writer put his finger in the alphabet soup?
Tommy: He was searching for the right words.

Customer: Waiter, waiter, do the band play requests?
Waiter: Yes, Sir.
Customer: Well, then — ask them to play cards until I've finished my lunch.

Customer: Waiter, waiter, your tie is in my soup!
Waiter: That's all right, Sir — it won't shrink.

Customer: Waiter, waiter, a dog just ran off with my steak!
Waiter: Yes, Sir — it's very popular.

Customer: Waiter, waiter, there's a worm on my plate.
Waiter: No, Sir — that's the sausage.

Customer: Waiter, waiter, if this is cod, I'm a fool!
Waiter: That's right, Sir — it *is* cod.

Customer: Waiter, waiter, the food in this restaurant is awful. Bring me the manager.
Waiter: I'm sorry, Sir — he's out to lunch.

Customer: Waiter, waiter, today I'd like my soup without.
Waiter: Without what, Sir?
Customer: Without your thumb in it.

When was beef at its highest ever price?
When the cow jumped over the moon.

Customer: Waiter, waiter, this egg is bad.
Waiter: Don't blame me, Sir — I only laid the table.

What is orange, long, and shoots rabbits?
A double-barrelled carrot.

Customer: Waiter, waiter, there's a flea in my soup.
Waiter: Shall I tell him to hop it, Sir?

Customer: Waiter, waiter, what's the meaning of this fly in my teacup?
Waiter: I'm a waiter, Sir — not a fortune teller.

Customer: Waiter, waiter, I'd like a table for dinner.
Waiter: Certainly, Sir — boiled, roasted or fried?

Customer: Waiter, waiter, there's a fly in my butter!
Waiter: There can't be, Sir.
Customer: I'm telling you there's a fly in my butter!
Waiter: That's impossible, Sir — we only use margarine.

Why should you never tell secrets in a wheat field?
Because corn has ears.

Timmy: I eat lots of spinach because it puts colour in my cheeks.
Nick: Who wants green cheeks!

Customer: Waiter, waiter, what's this in my soup?
Waiter: I've no idea, Sir — I can't tell one insect from another.

What is an extra-long hot dog called?
A frankfurther.

Customer: Waiter, waiter, what is this soup?
Waiter: It's bean soup, Sir.
Customer: I don't care what it's been — what is it now?

Customer: Waiter, waiter, there's a fly in my soup.
Waiter: Don't worry, Sir — the spider on your bread roll will get it.

Customer: Waiter, waiter, this coffee is very weak!
Waiter: What do you want me to do, Sir — give it weight training?

What happened when there was a fight in the fish and chip shop?
A lot of fish got battered.

What is white outside, green inside, and hops?
A frog sandwich.

Customer: Waiter, waiter, I'd like a cup of coffee without cream.
Waiter: We're out of cream, Sir — would you like it without milk?

Is it true that carrots are good for the eyesight?
Well, you never see rabbits wearing glasses!

Customer: Waiter, waiter, I'd like my bill, please.
Waiter: Certainly Sir — how did you find your steak?
Customer: Oh, I just moved a chip and there it was.

Natasha: Once a week I take a milk bath.
Tommy: Pasteurized?
Natasha: No, only up to my neck.

Customer: Waiter, waiter, I can't eat this!
Waiter: Why not, Sir?
Customer: Because you haven't given me a knife and fork.

Customer: Waiter, waiter, I think I'd like a little game today.
Waiter: Certainly, Sir — chess or cards?

Customer: Waiter, waiter, what is this fly doing in my soup?
Waiter: Looks like the breast stroke to me, Sir.

Customer: Waiter, waiter, I'm in a hurry. Will the pancakes be long?
Waiter: No, Sir — round.

Waiter: We have practically everything on the menu, Sir.
Customer: So I see — bring me a clean one, please.

RIDICULOUS RIDDLES

We have had hundreds of riddles sent into us at WAC. Here are some of the most ridiculous.

What runs all around the garden without ever moving?
The fence.

How can you tell one sort of cat from another?
Look in the catalogue.

What plays when it works, and works when it plays?
A fountain.

Why is an island like the letter T?
Because it is in the middle of water.

From which number can you take half and leave nothing?
The number 8. Take away the top half and 0 is left.

When is a car not a car?
When it turns into a garage.

What is the best way to remove paint from a chair?
Sit down on it before it is dry.

What gets wetter the more it dries?
Your bath towel.

Why should you never tell a joke when you are ice skating?
Because the ice might crack up.

Timmy: How do you spell 'blind pig'?
Natasha: B-L-I-N-D P-I-G.
Timmy: No, B-L-N-D P-G. A blind pig has no eyes!

What can a whole apple do that half an apple
cannot?
It can look round.

What gives milk and says, 'Oom, oom'?
A cow walking backwards.

If two men dig a hole in five days, how many
days would it take them to dig half a hole?
None — you cannot dig half a hole.

What is a doughnut?
Someone who is crazy about money.

How long will an eight-day clock run without
winding?
It will not run at all without winding.

What does a dog get when it graduates?
A pedigree.

What can be right but can never be wrong?
An angle.

When is a sailor not a sailor?
When he is aboard.

Which creature becomes more healthy when it is beheaded?
The whale — because it becomes hale.

Why is U the happiest letter in the alphabet?
Because it is always in the middle of fun.

What nationality is Santa Claus?
North Polish.

Nick: Have you heard the story about the 'flu germ?
Tommy: No, what's the story?
Nick: Never mind, I don't want to spread it around.

What does a caterpillar do on New Year's Day?
He turns over a new leaf.

What is the best thing out?
An aching tooth.

With which vegetable do you throw away the outside, then cook the inside, eat the outside and then throw away the inside?
Corn on the cob.

Where is everyone equally beautiful?
In the dark.

What is the difference between a crazy rabbit and a counterfeit coin?
One is a mad bunny, the other is bad money.

What ship is always managed by more than one person?
A partnership.

How do you get down from an elephant?
You do not get down from an elephant — you get down from a duck.

What can run but cannot walk?
Water.

Gyles: Why is a Christmas pudding like the ocean?
Arabella: I don't know, why is a Christmas pudding like the ocean?
Gyles: Because it's full of currants.

What has a head but no brain, yet still drives?
A golf club.

Which is the strongest day of the week?
Sunday — because all the rest are weekdays.

How do you make notes out of stone?
Rearrange the letters.

What is a boxer's favourite drink?
Punch.

Who is the strongest thief in the world?
A shoplifter.

Why is that you always find something in the last place you look?
Because when you find it, you stop looking.

When is it right to say 'I is'?
When you say, 'I is the letter which comes after H.'

What can be measured, but has no length, no width and no thickness?
The temperature.

What gets harder to catch the faster you run?
Your breath.

What turns everything round but never moves?
A mirror.

Why does the stork stand on one leg?
Because if it lifted the other one it would fall over.

Why can't a deaf man be sent to prison?
Because you cannot condemn a man without a hearing.

What is oil before it is discovered?
A well-kept secret.

Why is a poor friend better than a rich one?
Because a friend in need is a friend indeed.

Natasha: Have you heard the story about the peacock?
James: Yes! What a beautiful tail!

Why did the Romans build straight roads?
Because they did not want to drive their soldiers round the bend.

Why can't it rain for two nights in a row?
Because there is a day in between.

What has a neck but no head?
A bottle.

What do you lose every time you stand up?
Your lap.

What is very light but can never be lifted?
A bubble.

What always stays hot, even if you put it in the
refrigerator?
Mustard.

What goes up and never comes down?
Your age.

Sally: Which animal never plays fair?
Nick: I don't know — which animal never plays
fair?
Sally: The cheetah!

What is the best way to double your money?
Fold it in half.

What is always down even when it flies in the
air?
A feather.

What can you hold without touching it?
A conversation.

The more there is of it, the less you see. What is
it?
Darkness.

What has four fingers and a thumb, but neither
flesh nor bone?
A glove.

As long as I eat, I live — but when I drink, I die.
What am I?
A fire.

GHOSTS, MONSTERS AND LEGENDS

A spooktacular chapter this — full of eerie rib-ticklers and ghastly ghostly giggles . . .

How do worried ghosts look?
Grave.

Why are vampires mad?
Because they are often bats.

What do ghosts call their Navy?
The Ghost-Guard.

What do you call a monster that has no luck?
The Luck Less Monster.

Who appears on the cover of horror
magazines?
The cover ghoul.

How do you flatten a ghost?
With a spirit level.

Which ghost has the best hearing?
The eeriest.

Arabella: I met a zombie last night.
James: What did it say?
Arabella: I don't know — I can't speak dead languages.

What do you call a skeleton that never dances?
Lazy bones.

What happened to the boy who slept with his head under his pillow?
The fairies took all his teeth out.

What do witches give their guests to eat?
Pot luck.

How can you tell a monster from an elephant?
A monster never remembers.

How do monsters count to fifty-three?
On their fingers.

What is a gargoyle?
Something spooks take when they have a sore throat.

Who has feathers, fangs, and goes 'quack'?
Count Duckula.

How does Frankenstein eat his food?
He bolts it down.

What do you call a ghost doctor?
A surgical spirit.

Where do ghosts get their jokes from?
Crypt writers.

1st monster: That girl over there just rolled her eyes at me.
2nd monster: Well, roll them back; she might need them.

Why can't skeletons fight?
They haven't the stomach for it.

How do wc know that ghosts are simple things?
Because we can see through them so easily.

What is a nightmare?
A horse that goes to bed very late.

Why was the Egyptian boy sad?
Because his daddy was a mummy.

Why did Frankenstein see a psychiatrist?
Because he thought everybody loved him.

How does a ghoul start a letter?
Tomb it may concern.

Gyles: What would you do if a ghost floated in through your front door?
Sally: I'd run out of the back door!

What is a ghost's favourite foreign food?
Spookhetti.

'Mum, what's a vampire?'
'Be quiet! And drink up your soup before it clots.'

What is the difference between a musician and a corpse?
One composes while the other decomposes.

Why do witches ride brooms?
Because vacuum cleaners are too heavy.

What has a black cape, crawls through the night, and bites people?
A tired mosquito with a black cape.

Why do little witches always get A's at school?
Because they are very good at spelling.

How can you tell if someone has a glass eye?
When it comes out in conversation.

What did one invisible man say to the other invisible man?
'It's nice not to see you again.'

Who does a fiend see every Saturday night?
His girl fiend.

What is the name of a ghost's favourite pub?
The Horse and Gloom.

What did the cannibal say when he saw the missionary asleep?
Ah, breakfast in bed.

Who comes out at night and goes, 'Munch, munch, ouch!'
A vampire with toothache.

Why did the Cyclops stop teaching?
Because he only had one pupil.

Why did the boy spook push his father's finger into the electric light socket?
Because he wanted fizzy pop.

What is a ghost's favourite dessert?
Leeches and scream.

What do you call a beautiful, polite monster?
A failure.

Why do monsters always forget everything you tell them?
Because it goes in one ear and out the others.

Why is it dangerous to sleep on a train?
Because trains run over sleepers.

Tommy: I once knew this horrible man who had snoo in his blood.
Sally: Sounds awful! What's snoo?
Tommy: Not a lot. What's new with you?

What did the monster eat after the dentist took all his teeth out?
The dentist.

Which day of the week do spooks like best?
Moanday.

What is Dracula's favourite society?
The Consumers' Association.

What would you call something with two mouths, three noses, and four eyes?
Very, very ugly.

What do you get when you have your head chopped off?
A splitting headache.

How do vampires travel?
By blood vessel.

'Doctor, do my X-rays show that I'm quite normal?'
'Oh, yes. Both your heads are perfectly all right.'

Why do ghosts like tall buildings?
Because there are so many scarecases.

What do undertakers die from?
Coffin.

What do you get if you cross a ghost with a packet of crisps?
Snacks that go crunch in the night.

Why do dead people never arrive in heaven on time?
Because they have to be 'late' to get there.

1st cannibal: I don't know what to make of my husband.
2nd cannibal: How about a hotpot?

James: One of my ancestors was killed at Waterloo.
Arabella: Oh, really? Which platform?

'Daddy, daddy, I don't want to go to Australia.'
'Shut up, son, and keep swimming.'

What did Frankenstein say when he was struck by lightning?
Thanks! I feel much better for that.

KNOCK, KNOCK

Knock, knock.
Who's there?
A chap.
A chap who?
A chap-ter full of Knock Knock jokes!

Knock, knock.
Who's there?
Teresa.
Teresa who?
Teresa Green.

Knock, knock.
Who's there?
Datsun.
Datsun who?
Datsun old joke.

Knock, knock.
Who's there?
Iowa.
Iowa who?
Iowa lot of money to the Inland Revenue.

Knock, knock.
Who's there?
Cook.
Cook who?
Oh! That's the first one I've heard this year.

Knock, knock.
Who's there?
Zookeeper.
Zookeeper who?
Zookeeper way from me if you've got the flu.

Knock, knock.
Who's there?
Thumping.
Thumping who?
Thumping green and slimy is crawling up your sleeve.

Knock, knock.
Who's there?
Tyrone.
Tyrone who?
Tyrone shoe laces — you're old enough now.

Knock, knock.
Who's there?
Bernadette.
Bernadette who?
Bernadette all my dinner.

Knock, knock.
Who's there?
Yelp.
Yelp who?
Yelp me! I've got my nose stuch in the keyhole.

Knock, knock.
Who's there?
Cantaloupe.
Cantaloupe who?
We cantaloupe tonight — my parents are watching.

Knock, knock.
Who's there?
Acid.
Acid who?
Acid down and shut up!

Knock, knock.
Who's there?
Arthur.
Arthur who?
Arthur any biscuits left?

Knock, knock.
Who's there?
Sarah.
Sarah who?
Sarah doctor in the house?

Knock, knock.
Who's there?
Cows.
Cows who?
Cows go 'moo', 'not 'who'.

Knock, knock.
Who's there?
Little old lady.
Little old lady who?
I didn't know you could yodel!

Knock, knock.
Who's there?
Snow.
Snow who?
Snow use — I've forgotten my name again.

Knock, knock.
Who's there?

Tuba.
Tuba who?
Tuba toothpaste, please.

Knock, knock.
Who's there?
Doughnut.
Doughnut who?
Doughnut ask silly questions — just open the door.

Knock, knock.
Who's there?
Iris.
Iris who?
Iris you were here.

Knock, knock.
Who's there?

Oswald.
Oswald who?
Oswald my bubble gum.

Knock, knock.
Who's there?
Shirley.
Shirley who?
Shirley you must know by now!

Knock, knock.
Who's there?
Howie.
Howie who?
I'm okay — how are you?

Knock, knock.
Who's there?
Romeo.
Romeo who?
Romeover to the other side of the lake and then
I'll tell you.

Knock, knock.
Who's there?
Juno.
Juno who?
Juno what time it is?

Knock, knock.
Who's there?
Godfrey.
Godfrey who?
Godfrey tickets for the circus tonight!

Knock, knock.
Who's there?
Luke.
Luke who?
Luke through the keyhole and you'll see.

Knock, knock.
Who's there?
Felix.
Felix who?
Felix my lollipop again, I'll hit him.

Knock, knock.
Who's there?
Harvey.
Harvey who?
Harvey going to play this game together?

Knock, knock.
Who's there?

Tank.
Tank who?
You're welcome.

Knock, knock.
Who's there?
Alex.
Alex who?
Alex the questions, if you don't mind.

Knock, knock.
Who's there?
Howard.
Howard who?
Howard you know if you don't open the door?

Knock, knock.
Who's there?
Walter.
Walter who?
Walter wall carpets.

Knock, knock.
Who's there?
Hurd.
Hurd who?
Hurd my hand knocking on this door.

Knock, knock.
Who's there?
Buster.
Buster who?
Buster the sports stadium, please.

Knock, knock.
Who's there?
Eileen.
Eileen who?
Eileen'd on your fence and broke it.

Knock, knock.
Who's there?
Ya.
Ya who?
I never knew you were a cowboy!

Knock, knock.
Who's there?
Danielle.
Danielle who?
Danielle so loud! We can hear you.

Knock, knock.
Who's there?

Fred.
Fred who?
Fred this needle for me, please.

Knock, knock.
Who's there?
Police.
Police who?
Police open the door so I can come in.

Knock, knock.
Who's there?
Noah.
Noah who?
Noah anywhere to eat around here?

Knock, knock.
Who's there?
Barbara.
Barbara who?
Barbara black sheep, have you any wool?

Knock, knock.
Who's there?
Arch.
Arch who?
Bless you!

Knock, knock.
Who's there?
Zoom.

Zoom who?
Zoom are you expecting?
Knock, knock.
Who's there?
Minnie.
Minnie who?
No, not Minnie who — Minnehaha.

Knock, knock.
Who's there?
Boo.
Boo who?
Just boo — I'm a ghost.

Knock, knock.
Who's there.
You.
You who?
You who! Is anybody home?

Knock, knock.
Who's there?
Miniature.
Miniature who?
Miniature open your mouth, you put your foot
in it.

Knock, knock.
Who's there?
Zsa Zsa.
Zsa Zsa who?
Zsa Zsa last knock, knock joke I want to hear!

BONK 'N' BOOB

On the Wide Awake Club BONK 'N' BOOB is our exciting high-speed spelling game. In the WAC Joke Book it is a chapter of ridiculous rib-ticklers and real classroom howlers. Everything marked BONK! should make you chuckle and everything marked BOOB! should make you groan because all the Boobs are actual mistakes made by real kids in the real skools!

BOOB!
A medicine ball is a dance for sick animals.

BONK!
Mother: How did the exams go at school today?
Were the questions easy?
Son: Oh, the questions were easy enough — it
was the answers I had trouble with.

BOOB!
An oxygen has eight sides.

BOOB!
A centimetre is an insect with a hundred legs.

BOOB!
A doggerell is a little dog.

BOOB!
Venison is an Italian city with lots of canals.

BONK!
Why did the teacher marry the caretaker?
Because he swept her off her feet.

BOOB!
Monsoon is a French word meaning 'Mr'.

BONK!
Natasha: Why did the schoolboy stand on his head?
Tommy: I don't know — why did the schoolboy stand on his head?
Natasha: So that he could turn things over in his head.

BONK!
How did the schoolgirl know that when her chemistry teacher dropped a pound coin into a jar of acid it would not dissolve?
Because if the coin was going to dissolve, the teacher would never have dropped it in.

BONK!
Why was Goliath surprised when David hit him
with a stone?
It had never entered his head before.

BONK!
What is the definition of an abnormal pupil?
**One who remembers to bring his homework
back after the holidays?**

BONK!
Mother: How was your first day at school?
Daughter: First day? Do you mean I have to go
back tomorrow?

BONK!
What is an expert? Well, if X is a mathematical
term, meaning unknown, and a spurt is a drip
under pressure, an expert must be an unknown
drip under pressure.

BONK!
Teacher: When we go into the playground on a
cold winter's day, what do we see on every
hand?
Pupil: Gloves.

BONK!
The more we study, the more we know.
The more we know, the more we forget.
The more we forget, the less we know.
So — why study?

BOOB!
Bamboo was a little fawn in a Disney cartoon.

BOOB!
Noah's wife was Joan of Arc.

BONK!
Timmy: Who wrote *To A Field Mouse*?
Gyles: I've no idea — but I bet he didn't get a reply!

BOOB!
Teacher: How can you prove that the world is round?
Pupil: I never said it was!

BONK!
What happened to the plant in the mathematics class?
It grew square roots.

BONK!
What do Zulus do with banana skins?
Throw them away!

BONK!
What are the three most popular words at school?
I don't know.

BOOB!
Macaroni was the inventor of the radio.

BOOB!
When a dog has puppies it is called a litre.

BONK!
Teacher: Why are you so late?
Pupil: Well, on my way I saw the sign which said,
'Go slow — school ahead'.

BOOB!
An atom is the man who lived in the Garden of
Eden with Eve.

BOOB!
Teacher: Why are the Dark Ages so called?
Pupil: Because they had so many knights.

BONK!
What would you have if you lost four fingers in an accident?
No more piano lessons.

BONK!
What examinations does Santa Claus take?
Ho! Ho! Ho! Levels.

BONK!
Did you hear about the cross-eyed teacher who could not control her pupils?

BOOB!
Poetry is when every line starts with a capital letter.

BONK:
Arabella: Did your school music teacher ever say your voice was heavenly?
Tommy: Not exactly — she used to say it was like nothing on earth.

BOOB!
Letters in sloping type are called hysterics.

BONK!
Teacher: Which month has twenty-eight days?
Pupil: They all have!

BOOB!
Tom Sawyer was smart; his character was always good sometimes.

BOOB!
Teacher: Name three collective nouns.
Pupil: Dustpan, rubbish bin and vacuum cleaner.

BOOB!
Dusk is the fluff that you find under your bed.

BONK!
Where does satisfaction come from?
A satisfactory.

BONK!
Why did the little girl cut a hole in her umbrella?
So that she could see when it had stopped raining.

BOOB!
A silverfish is an imitation goldfish.

BONK!
Teacher: If you had ten pence in one pocket, and ten pence in your other pocket, what would you have?
Pupil: Someone else's coat.

BONK!
What is the difference between a teacher and a train?
A teacher says, 'Spit out that gum!' and a train says, 'Chew-chew!'

BONK!
Teacher: Why is your essay on milk so short? Everyone else in class has written two pages, and you've only written two lines!
Pupil: That's because I wrote about condensed milk.

BOOB!
A ruminating animal chews its cubs.

BONK!
Pupil: I don't think I deserve nought for my homework!
Teacher: Nor do I — but it's the lowest mark I can give you.

BONK!
What happens to pupils who think that electricity is easy?
They get quite a shock!

BOOB!
The future of 'I give' is 'You take'.

BONK!
Teacher: I hope you all made someone happy over the weekend.
Pupil: Oh, I did! I spent Saturday with my auntie, and when I left she was happy.

BOOB!
Vandals are open-toed shoes that we wear in the summer.

BOOB!
Teacher: Name a liquid that cannot freeze.
Pupil: Hot water.

BOOB!
Quadrupeds has no singular . . . have you ever
seen a one-legged horse?

BONK!
Why did the germ cross the microscope?
To get to the other side.

BOOB!
Impassable is a wet football.

BOOB!
'*Coup*' is the French word for chicken-house.

BONK!
Teacher: What causes trees to become petrified?
Pupil: The wind makes them rock.

BOOB!
A hostage is a kind lady on an aeroplane.

BONK!
What is the difference between lightning and
electricity?
We have to pay for electricity!

BONK!
Teacher: I asked you to draw a horse and cart,
and you've only drawn the horse!
Pupil: Well, I thought the horse could draw the
cart.

THE WAC ALL STARS

We like to think that Tommy and Arabella and James (and even Gyles) are the real WAC All Stars, but in this chapter we thought we'd let some other World Famous Personalities take the stage . . .

James: Why do you suppose King Arthur had a round table?
Nick: He probably didn't want to get cornered.

What were Tarzan's last words?
Who greased the vine?

How do we know that Prince Charles was a cry-baby when he was small?
Because he is called the Prince of Wales.

What does Kojak write with?
A bald-point pen.

What famous detective loved bubble baths?
Sherlock Foams.

Why wouldn't they let Cinderella play hockey?
Because she kept running away from the ball.

For how long did Cain hate his brother?
For as long as he was Abel.

Who was the biggest bandit in history?
Atlas—he held up the world.

What do you call an Egyptian Pharaoh that eats
biscuits in its tomb?
A crummy mummy.

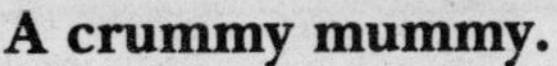

If kings like to sit on gold, who likes to sit on
silver?
The Lone Ranger.

What kind of corsage did Lassie used to wear?
A collie flower.

Why couldn't anyone find the famous composer?
Because he was Haydn.

Why was the Duke of Wellington late for the battle?
Because his boots were on the wrong foot.

How many letters are there in the alphabet?
Twenty-four—ET's gone home.

Timmy: I hear John McEnroe's going to star in a new film.
Sally: Oh, what's it called?
Timmy: The Umpire Strikes Back.

The thunder god went for a ride on his favourite horse and cried out, 'I'm Thor!' The horse replied, 'You forgot your thaddle, thilly!'

Where did Sir Lancelot study?
At Knight School.

What bus crossed the ocean?
Columbus.

How many ears has Captain Kirk got?
Three—a right ear, a left ear, and a final frontier!

Where did Napoleon keep his armies?
Up his sleevies.

Why did Mickey Mouse go on a space shuttle trip?
Because he wanted to find Pluto.

Why was Batman sad in the autumn?
Because Robin flew south.

Who was the straightest man in the Bible?
Joseph, because King Pharaoh made a ruler out of him.

What is green and holds up stage coaches?
Dick Gherkin.

Natasha: Who invented the fireplace?
Nick: I don't know — who invented the fireplace?
Natasha: Alfred the Grate, of course!

Where was Michael Jackson when the lights went out?
In the dark.

How does Jack Frost get to work?
By icicle.

What is the first mention of medicine in the Bible?
When God gave Moses two tablets.

What is the difference between Joan of Arc and Noah's Ark?
One is Maid of Orleans and the other is made of wood.

Why didn't Robin Hood ever rob the poor?
Because they didn't have much worth taking.

Why did the chicken cross the road?
To get away from Colonel Sanders.

What do you get if you cross a cowboy with a nourishing meal?
Hopalong Casserole.

Why is Prince William like a cloudy day?
Because he is likely to reign.

What lurks at the bottom of the sea and makes you an offer you cannot refuse?
The Codfather.

What promise did Adam and Eve make when they were thrown out of the Garden of Eden?
That they would turn over a new leaf.

Arabella: When did Caesar reign?
James: I didn't know he rained.
Arabella: Of course he did — didn't they hail him?

What does Her Majesty the Queen do when she burps?
She issues a Royal Pardon.

Tommy: Do you believe in fate?
Gyles: I'm not sure, why?
Tommy: Well, haven't you ever wondered why all famous people were born on holidays?

Two flies were sitting on Robinson Crusoe's knee. 'Bye for now,' said one. 'I'll see you on Friday.'

What did Benjamin Franklin say when he discovered electricity?
Nothing — he was too shocked.

Why is Prince Henry like the post?
Because he is a Royal Male.

What language does Jacques Cousteau speak?
Fluid French.

Romeo: Juliet, my love, I'm burning with love for you.
Juliet: Oh, Romeo, don't make a fuel of yourself!

How do we know that Moses wore a wig?
Because sometimes he was seen with Aaron and sometimes without.

Autograph hunter: Haven't I seen your face somewhere else?
Football star: I don't think so — it's always been between my ears.

Who took Little Bo Peep's sheep?
The crook she had with her.

What would you get if you crossed Boy George with a fire-breathing monster?
The Georgian Dragon.

What was Winston Churchill famous for?
His memory — after all, they erected a statue to it.

Interviewer: Excuse my asking, but what are those little bongos hanging from your ears?
Madonna: Oh, those are just my ear-drums.

Who was the fastest runner in history?
Adam — because he was first in the human race.

What happened when Popeye tried to cook a pizza?
There was Olive Oyl over the place.

Arthur Scargill broke his nose and went to see the doctor, who said, 'Try not to picket for a few weeks.'

1st lady with pram: I'm going to call my baby Orson, after Orson Welles.
2nd lady with pram: What's your surname?
1st lady with pram: Cart.

What do you call a man dressed in two raincoats standing in a cemetery?
Max Bygraves.

Did you know that it was Anne Hathaway who named William Shakespeare's play *Julius Caesar*? He originally wanted to call it *Julius, Grab the Girl Quickly Before She Gets Away.*

Of course you know that you cannot send a letter to Washington — because he is dead. But you *can* send a letter to Lincoln — because he left his Gettysburg Address.

What is purple and conquered the world?
Alexander the Grape.

When is tennis mentioned in the Bible?
When Joseph served in Pharaoh's court.

VERSE — AND WORSE!

If you like potty poetry and ridiculous rhymes, you will love this chapter. The poetry here is as potty and ridiculous as it comes!

During dinner at the Ritz
Father kept on having fits.
And, which made my sorrow greater,
I was left to tip the waiter.

I wish I had your picture.
It would be very nice.
I'd hang it in the cellar
To scare away the mice!

Don't worry if your job is small
And your rewards are few.
Remember that the mighty oak
Was once a nut like you!

I shot an arrow in the air.
It fell to earth, I know not where.
I lose all my arrows that way.

Ding dong bell.
Pussy's in the well.

But we've put some disinfectant down,
And don't care about the smell.

Mary had a little lamb,
Her father shot it dead.
And now it goes to school with her
Between two chunks of bread.

A spook stood on the bridge one night,
Its lips were all a-quiver.
It gave a cough,
Its leg fell off
And floated down the river.

I love you, I love you,
Please be my Valentine.
And give me your bubble gum,
'Cos you're sitting on mine!

I shot a sneeze into the air.
It fell to earth, I know not where.
But some time later, so I'm told,
Twenty others caught my cold.

There was a young lady named Perkins
Who was so very fond of gherkins.
    One day at tea,
    She ate fifty-three
And pickled her internal workings.

Roses are red,
Violets are blue.
Sugar is sweet
And expensive too.

Dr Bell fell down a well
And broke his collar bone.
Doctors should attend the sick
And leave the well alone.

A flea and a fly in a flue
Were imprisoned, so what could they do?
Said the fly, 'Let us flee!'
Said the flea, 'Let us fly!'
So they flew through a flaw in the flue.

There was a young lady from Gloucester
Whose parents thought they had lost her.
From the fridge came a sound
And at last she was found,
But the problem was how to defrost her!

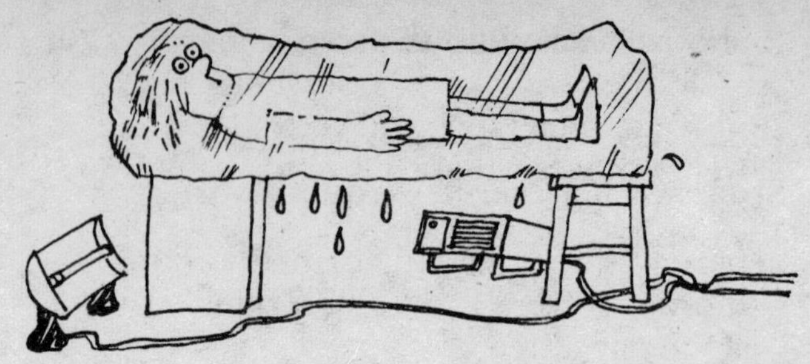

If we forget then we've forgotten,
But things we wet are never wotten,
And houses let cannot be lotten.

The baker's wife, Alberta Smythe,
Had loads and loads of fun,
For every time she did her hair
She put it in a bun.

While shepherds washed their socks by night,
All seated round the tub,
The angel of the Lord came down
And joined the rub-a-dub.

History's an awful subject,
As dead as dead can be.
It killed the ancient Romans,
And now it's killing me.

There was a young lady named Rose
Who had a huge wart on her nose.
When she had it removed
Her appearance improved

But her glasses slipped down to her toes.

Last night I slew my wife,
Stretched her on the parquet flooring.
I was loth to take her life —
But I had to stop her snoring.

There was an old man known as Keith,
Who sat on his set of false teeth.
Said he with a start,
'Oh dear, bless my heart!
I have bitten myself underneath!'

When I die, bury me deep,
Bury my chemistry book at my feet.

Tell the teacher I've gone to rest,
And won't be there for the chemistry test.

Happy Birthday to you,
Squashed tomatoes and stew.
You look like a monkey,
And you act like one too!

Little Billy late one night
Lit a stick of dynamite.
Don't you think he had a cheek?
It's been raining Billy for a week.

The horse bit his master,
How came this to pass?
He heard the good Pastor
Say, 'All flesh is grass!'

The sausage is a clever bird,
Its feathers bright and wavy.
It swims about the frying pan
And nests amongst the gravy.

Humpty Dumpty sat on a wall,
Humpty Dumpty had a great fall,
All the king's horses and all the king's men
Had scrambled egg again.

Here lies a boy who played the fool,
When coming home one day from school.
He forgot his highway code,
What happened next, he never knowed.

I eat my peas with honey,
I've done it all my life.
It may seem kind of funny,
But it keeps them on my knife.

The wonderful Wizard of Oz
Retired from business becoz
What with up-to-date science,
To most of his clients
He wasn't the wiz that he woz.

'Your teeth are like the stars,' he said,
And pressed her hand so white.
He spoke the truth, for like the stars,
Her teeth came out at night.

A well-built old fellow named Skinner
Said, 'How I wish I were thinner!'
He lived for three weeks
On a grape and two leeks —
We think of him, Sundays, at dinner.

Billy, in his nice new sash,
Fell in the fire and was burnt to ash,
Now, although the room grows chilly,
I haven't the heart to poke poor Billy.

The rain makes all things beautiful,
The grass and flowers too.
If rains makes all things beautiful
Why don't it rain on you?

A cannibal bold of Penzance
Ate an uncle and two of his aunts,
A cow and her calf,
An ox and a half —
And now he can't button his pants.

It's easy enough to be pleasant
When life flows round and round,
But the man worthwhile
Is the man who can smile
With his trousers falling down!

Little Jack Horner sat in a corner
Eating his Christmas pie.
He put in his thumb, but instead of a plum,
He squirted fruit juice in his eye.

The reason she smiled — Mona Lisa —
Was seeing the Tower of Pisa.
They didn't quite mean
To make the thing lean,
But they built it that way just to please 'er.

Here I sit in the moonlight,
Abandoned by women and men,
Muttering over and over,
'I'll never eat garlic again!'

Early to bed
And early to rise
Makes you feel stupid
And gives you red eyes.

Down the street his funeral goes
As sobs and wails diminish,
He died from drinking varnish —
But what a lovely finish!

An incompetent sailor named Scott
Tried crossing the channel by yacht.
A storm blew him off course,
So he tapped out in Morse:
...---...

Mary had a little lamb
(You've heard this tale before),
But did you know she passed her plate
And had a little more?

A dog is loved
By old and young.
He wags his tail
And not his tongue.

Mother heard her children scream
So she pushed them in the stream,
Saying, as she pushed the third,
'Children should be seen, *not* heard.'

The night was growing dark and cold
As she trudged through snow and sleet;
And her nose was long and cold
And her shoes were full of feet.

If a man who 'Turnips!' cries

Cries not when his father dies,
Is it not proof he'd rather
Have a turnip than his father?

Jack and Jill went up the hill
To fetch a pail of water.
Jack fell down and broke his crown,
And sued the farmer and his daughter.

When accepting a young man at Kew,
A maiden said, 'Yes, I'll be true.
But you must understand,
As you've asked for my hand,
That the rest of me goes with it too!'

Sweet Little Eileen Rose
Was tired and sought some sweet repose.
But her naughty sister Clare
Placed a pin upon her chair
And sweet little Eileen rose!

CRAZY GRAFFITI

At WAC we are dead against graffiti that gets scrawled on walls — but we like fun slogans and crazy messages, so here are some of our favourites. Every one is genuine.

It is dangerous to swim on a full stomach —
Swim on your back instead.

If you cannot communicate — try talking.

Happiness is a blank white wall.

What can I take for kleptomania?

A broken leg is not what it's cracked up to be.

Keep Britain Tidy — post your rubbish abroad.

I hate being in the air in a plane —
I'd hate to be in the air without one.

I don't care if I win or lose, as long as I win.

Laugh and the world laughs with you —
But you'll be asked to leave the Library.

Do unto others before they get a chance to do it
unto you.

Cowardice rules — if that's all right with all of
you.

The Venus de Milo is perfectly armless.

If you can't read — just watch this space.

Drums take a lot of beating.

I can only afford to go window shopping —
How many windows did you buy?

The only good books are read ones.

Is there intelligent life on earth?
Yes, but I'm only visiting.

Is clumsiness catching?
No, only dropping.

Every day has its day —
But only a dog with a broken tail has a weak
end.

Tolkein is Hobbit-forming.

I used to be undecided — but now I'm not so sure.

A friend in need is a pest.

Do chickens get people pox?

The best way to talk to a lion is by long-distance telephone.
Sorry — lion's busy.

Give karate the chop.

Give ants a break — walk on one leg.

Do Vikings use Norse code?

I scored five goals on Saturday!
Pity they were all own goals.

Free the Inter-City 125.

Don't lose any sleep over insomnia.

Hypochondriacs make me sick.

Down with gravity.

Bite a fisherman — it might be the only one he
gets all day.

Van Gogh was ear.

Is an asset a little donkey?

My teacher loves me — she puts kisses on all my
sums.

The paper shop just blew away.

I'm the biggest liar in the world —
I don't believe you.

Don't play in the street — you may get that run
down feeling.

Flowers rule — bouquet.

An elephant never forgets —
But what has he got to remember?

SHORT-SIGHTED PEOPLE RULE OK.

No problem is so big you cannot run away from
it.

Our needlework teacher is a real sew and sew!

Only dirty people need to wash.

Do not write on these walls —
Print.

Lightning cannot conduct itself.

Be aloof — the country has enough lerts.

Legalize telepathy! —
I knew you were going to say that.

Shoplifters have the gift of the grab.

Modern music is not as bad as it sounds.

You can always count on your fingers.

Do moon beams hold the moon up in the sky?

Those who think they know it all are annoying
to those of us who do!

If you can't spell — consult a dikshunary.

I've lived on earth all my life —
Personally, I'd rather eat food.

Dracula is a pain in the neck.

Who was Corporal Punishment?

Can anybody help me out?
Which way did you come in?

I hate graffiti —
I hate all foreign food.

DOCTOR PETE, DOCTOR PETE!

Doctor Pete is the Wide Awake Club doctor. He is a real doctor. Sensible too — most of the time. Sometimes though, he does get a little silly . . .

Doctor Pete, Doctor Pete! I think I'm invisible.
Who said that?

Doctor Pete, Doctor Pete! I keep thinking I'm a
dustbin.
Don't talk rubbish.

Doctor Pete, Doctor Pete! I think I'm a goat.
How long have you thought this?
Oh, since I was a kid.

Doctor Pete, Doctor Pete! I think I'm a pair of
curtains.
Pull yourself together, man.

Doctor Pete, Doctor Pete! I feel like a pound
coin.
Go shopping — the change will do you good.

Doctor Pete, Doctor Pete! I think I'm a spoon.
Sit down and don't stir.

Doctor Pete, Doctor Pete! My hair is falling out.
Can you suggest anything to keep it in?
How about a carrier bag?

Doctor Pete, Doctor Pete! I've lost my memory.
When did this happen?
When did what happen?

Doctor Pete, Doctor Pete! My little girl has
swallowed a pen. What can I do?
Use a pencil until I get there.

Doctor Pete, Doctor Pete! I've just swallowed a
sheep.

How do you feel?
Very ba-aa-aa-ad.

Doctor Pete, Doctor Pete! I can't get to sleep at
night.
**Lie on the edge of the bed — you'll soon drop
off.**

Doctor Pete, Doctor Pete! There's something
wrong with my stomach.
**Keep your coat buttoned up and nobody will
notice.**

Doctor Pete, Doctor Pete! Those strength pills
you gave me aren't doing me any good.
Why not?
I can't get the top off the bottle.

Doctor Pete, Doctor Pete! I feel like a yo-yo.
Sit down, sit down, sit down.

Doctor Pete, Doctor Pete! I think I'm a clock.
Well, don't get wound up about it.

Doctor Pete, Doctor Pete! I feel like a
raspberry.
You *are* in a jam, aren't you!

Doctor Pete, Doctor Pete! I can't stop myself
stealing things.
Have you taken anything for it?

Doctor Pete, Doctor Pete! I feel like a pack of
cards.
Sit down. I'll deal with you later.

Doctor Pete, Doctor Pete! I can't stop pulling
ugly faces.
That's not a serious problem.
But people with ugly faces don't like it.

Doctor Pete, Doctor Pete! I have a terrible
problem. Can you help me out?
Of course. Which way did you come in?

Doctor Pete, Doctor Pete! I feel like a snooker
ball.
Get to the back of the queue, please.

Doctor Pete, Doctor Pete! Will my measles be
better next week?
I never make rash promises.

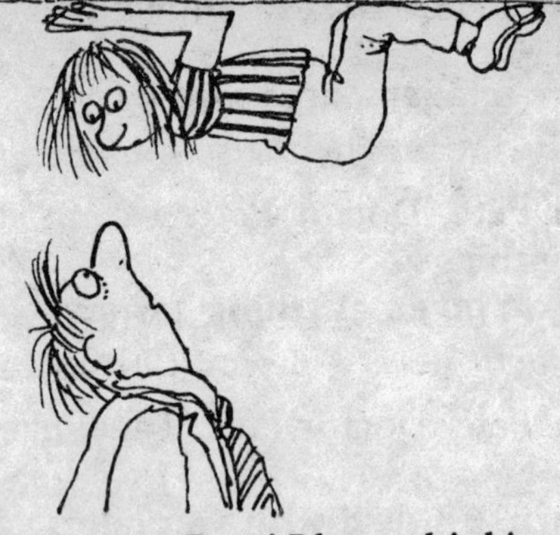

Doctor Pete, Doctor Pete! I keep thinking I'm a fly.
Come down off the ceiling and let's discuss it.

Doctor Pete, Doctor Pete! I'm having dreadful trouble with the contact lenses you gave me. I just can't get them over my glasses.

Doctor Pete, Doctor Pete! I think I'm a bird.
Perch over there, and I'll tweet you in a minute.

Doctor Pete, Doctor Pete! Everyone keeps ignoring me.
Next patient, please!

Doctor Pete, Doctor Pete! I'm so nervous — this is the first operation I've ever had.
Don't be nervous — this is the first operation I've ever performed.

Doctor Pete, Doctor Pete! You think I'm overweight, don't you?
Whatever makes you think that?
Well, during my check-up, you said, 'Open your mouth and say Moo-ooo . . .'

Doctor Pete, Doctor Pete! I think I'm an apple.
Come over here — I won't bite you.

Doctor Pete, Doctor Pete! I've got a very sore throat.
Just go over to the window and stick your tongue out.
Will that cure it?
No, I just don't like the woman who lives opposite the surgery.

Doctor Pete, Doctor Pete! I've got a bad liver. What shall I do?
Take it back to the butcher at once.

Doctor Pete, Doctor Pete! What's the best way to stop my nose running?
Stand on your head.

Doctor Pete, Doctor Pete! I'm having trouble with my breathing.
I'll see if I can give you something to stop that.

Doctor Pete, Doctor Pete! I keep thinking there

are two of me.
Don't both talk at once, please.

Doctor Pete, Doctor Pete! I can't seem to stop talking to myself
I wondered why you were looking so bored.

Doctor Pete, Doctor Pete! I get this feeling that nobody can hear what I'm saying.
What seems to be the trouble?

Doctor Pete, Doctor Pete! My wife thinks she's a car.
Show her in at once!
I can't do that — she's double-parked outside.

Doctor Pete, Doctor Pete! I just swallowed a mouth organ.
Think yourself lucky you don't play the piano!

Doctor Pete, Doctor Pete! I keep seeing double.
Lie on the couch, please.
Which one?

Doctor Pete, Doctor Pete! The banana diet you put me on is having very strange effects.
Stop scratching and come down from the curtains, would you?

Doctor Pete, Doctor Pete! I keep thinking I'm a ghost.
I wondered why you just walked in through the wall.

Doctor Pete, Doctor Pete! My husband thinks he's a duck.
Well, you'd better send him to see me.
I can't do that — he just flew south for the winter.

Doc-doc-ddd-Doctor Pete, Ddd-doc-ddd-Doctor Ppp-Pete! I-I-I ccc-ccc-can't sss-seem to get my words ooo-out.
Sorry, I wasn't listening. What did you say?

Doctor Pete, Doctor Pete! Are apples really healthy?
I've never heard one complain yet.

Doctor Pete, Doctor Pete! I feel funny — what should I do?
Go on television.

Doctor Pete, Doctor Pete! Last night I dreamed I ate a ten-pound marshmallow!
Don't worry — it was only a dream.
But when I woke up this morning my pillow was gone.

Doctor Pete, Doctor Pete! I've got potatoes growing out of my ears.
How on earth did that happen?
I don't know — I planted carrots.

Doctor Pete, Doctor Pete! I keep thinking I'm a bridge across The Thames.

Well, what has come over you today?

Doctor Pete, Doctor Pete! Everyone thinks I'm
a cricket ball.
How's that?
Oh, no! Not you as well!

Doctor Pete, Doctor Pete! I couldn't sleep a
wink last night.
Did you try counting sheep?
Yes, but when I got to 536,217 it was time to
get up.

Doctor Pete, Doctor Pete! I feel like an old
sock.
Well, I'll be darned.

Doctor Pete, Doctor Pete! I work like a horse,

eat like a bird and feel as tired as a dog.
Sounds like you need a vet, not a doctor.

Doctor Pete, Doctor Pete! I've swallowed a roll
of film.
Don't worry, nothing serious will develop.

Doctor Pete, Doctor Pete! I keep seeing yellow-
spotted elephants.
Have you ever seen a psychiatrist?
No, only yellow-spotted elephants.

Doctor Pete, Doctor Pete! I've swallowed a
mouse — what should I do?
Wave a piece of cheese in front of your mouth.

Doctor Pete, Doctor Pete! My husband thinks
he's a lift.
Bring him to see me, then.
I can't, he doesn't stop at your floor.

Doctor Pete, Doctor Pete! I've only got fifty-
nine seconds to live.
Come and sit down for a minute.

PRACTICAL JOKES

The WAC Joke Book proudly presents twenty-six of the world's silliest, safest, most stupendous Practical Jokes — all tried, tested and certified as terrific!

Shred up a sheet or two of newspaper. Unfurl an umbrella and place the shredded newspaper inside. Carefully roll up the umbrella and leave it, fastened, where you found it. Next time it is used, there will be a shower of 'confetti'!

Buy a few inexpensive bells — a good idea is to get the kind that hang in budgies' cages from a pet shop — and attach them with string to someone's bedsprings. When the person goes to bed they will hear a strange tinkling noise — and of course when they keep very still to try and discover where the noise is coming from, the noise will stop.

One of the oldest practical jokes is simply to balance a pillow on the top of a door which is slightly ajar. When the 'victim' pushes the door open and walks in, the pillow will fall on him or her!

Stand in the street with a friend and point up at the sky. If the two of you keep looking up and pointing you will soon be surrounded by a crowd!

Shake hands with friends when you met! Of course you will have put a spoonful of honey or butter in your palm first!

Ask a friend to write a small letter I with a dot over it. They will write 'i', which is wrong. A small letter I with a dot over it looks like: i .

Try turning all the clocks in the house back by an hour, so that when the cry goes up, 'Come on, time for bed!' you can point to a clock and say, 'But it's only six o'clock!' Your practical joke will of course be discovered before *too* long, but you will have had some extra time before going to bed.

Have you ever made an apple-pie bed? You need only use the bottom sheet, which you carefully fold about half-way along the bed. Tuck the blankets in in the normal way, turning the sheet over the top. An apple-pie bed is very difficult to get in to!

You could try sewing up your brother's or sister's pyjamas or nightdress, too! Just put a few stitches in the legs or arms, and make sure you are around to watch them hopping on one foot or waving their arms madly in the air as they try to get dressed for bed.

Next time you have boiled eggs for breakfast, secretly collect the empty eggshells, wash them and hide them away carefully. Then one morning when you offer to get the breakfast, you need only cook one egg for yourself, and put the empty eggshells upside down in the egg cups so that they look like the real thing!

A really spooky practical joke to play needs a little planning. Collect together an empty yoghurt pot or similar container, a few dried beans or peas and a metal tray. Fill the pot with the pulses, and just before someone in your house goes to bed, pour hot water into the pot. Stand the pot on the metal tray somewhere in the bedroom out of sight. As the water soaks into the peas they will expand and push the dried peas over the top of the pot so that they land on the tray making weird and wonderfully frightening noises.

Save an old newspaper and stick the pages together. You may have to wait a few days until the pages are really dry and completely stuck together. Then place these pages inside the front pages of today's newspaper. Watch what happens when someone tries to read the paper and cannot open the pages!

Try fooling your teacher! Tell her that someone in your family has a new hobby — they have taken up growing cacti, and have a unique specimen, which you are offering to take to school.

The joke is that you 'plant' a scouring pad in a pot of real earth, and unless your teacher is a real expert (in which case the joke is on you!) you could have her nurturing the plant for years!

Give a friend a 'pass the parcel' present for their birthday. Wrap up an old (preferably sprouting) potato in various boxes and layers of paper so that it takes ages to undo. When your friend looks suitably horrified at the old potato, you can give them their real present!

A very simple practical joke — but a very effective one — just uses a reel of cotton and a needle. Thread the needle, and push it through your jacket so that a short length is showing. You can keep the reel of cotton in your inside pocket. As soon as someone tries to remove the bit of cotton, you walk away as quickly as you can so that they are holding a bit of cotton that is getting longer with every step!

Take a piece of sticky tape and put it over the receiver rest of your telephone — under the receiver — so that it stays down when someone lifts the receiver. The next time the telephone is answered, someone is going to get the surprise of their life when the telephone keeps on ringing!

Write a message, such as 'Please Kiss Me' on a piece of paper and stick it on someone's back. Double-sided sticky tape is a good idea for this joke, and you can hide the message in your palm until you pat someone on the back in greeting them. If the joke works, they will spend all day wondering why they are so popular!

Another good joke to play with a coin, sticky tape and a piece of cotton — tape the cotton to the coin, lay the coin on the pavement and hide, holding the end of the cotton. As soon as someone bends down to pick up the coin, you jerk the cotton and the coin is instantly out of reach. But you will have to be quick, or you will lose your coin!

To 'measure a building' you need a long ball of string or a very long tape measure — and two 'victims'. Stand near the corner of a building, stop a passer-by and explain that you are measuring the building. Ask him to hold one end of the string while you walk around the corner, unravelling the string as you go. Once out of sight, ask another victim to hold the other end of the string. Then *you* go off to a spot where you can observe their reactions without yourself being seen. How long do you think it would be before they see who is on the other end of the string — or give up?

Try glueing a coin to the pavement with some extra strong glue. Hide where you cannot be seen, and have some fun watching people stoop down and try to pick it up!

Write the word WHAT on a piece of paper, and put it in your pocket. Then say to a friend, 'I know what you're going to say next!' They're bound to say, 'What?' and you simply take out your piece of paper and show it to them, saying, 'I told you I knew what you'd say next!'

Ask your father why he dropped a £5 note in amongst the old newspapers or garden rubbish. Of course, he will go hunting amongst everything to try to find it! This is a good practical joke to play on April Fool's Day!

Here is a joke you can play when there are walnuts in the house — perhaps at Christmas time. Break one of the nuts very carefully down the centre — it should fall perfectly in two halves. Remove the nut and replace it with anything that will fit — a marble, a coin, a peanut. Stick the two halves of the shell together with a small dab of glue and put the nut back in with the others. Then sit back and wait for someone to open it and watch the surprise on their faces!

Do you ever offer to wash up at home? Well, before you do next time, collect as many small metal objects as you can — ring pulls, spoons, tin lids, and so on. Then make sure you are alone in the kitchen and after a few minutes drop your collection on the floor, shouting, 'Oh-oh!'

When you next say goodbye to a friend, let him or her get a few metres away, and then call them back. As they ask what it is you want, whisper, 'How far would you have got if I hadn't called you back?' If he or she is cycling away, you could call out, 'Do you know your front wheel's going round?'

Offer a reward for your missing 'pet' — but make sure that you tell everyone it is a very special animal. Write out little notes and pop them through your neighbours' doors, you could choose a one-eyed camel, a two-headed dog, or just a pink cat! You will be surprised how many people are *sure* they have seen it!

THE WORST IN THE WORLD!

That is what we say. What do you say?

What are musicians supposed to wear?
Cords.

What is black, out of its mind and sits in trees?
A raven lunatic.

How can you avoid falling hair?
Jump out of the way.

What was the sheep doing on the motorway?
A ewe-turn.

What bird is always out of breath?
A puffin.

What makes people shy?
Coconuts.

What is the quickest way to the station?
Run like crazy.

What makes the Tower of Pisa lean?
Because it never eats.

If tyres hold up cars, what holds up an aeroplane?
Hijackers.

What is the best place for water skiing?
A lake with a slope.

When is a fountain like a biscuit tin?
When it is a square tin.

Why did the fish blush?
Because the sea weed.

Why did the biscuit cry?
Because its mother had been a wafer so long.

Which animal drives a car?
A road hog.

Why are tall people lazy?
Because they lie longer in bed.

What do disc jockeys wear?
A track suit.

What is the expression on an auctioneer's face?
For bidding.

What did one toe say to the other?
Look out! Two heels are following us.

How should you dress on a cold day?
Very quickly.

Who invented spaghetti?
Someone who used his noodle.

What do you call mad fleas?
Loony ticks.

How would you scold an elephant?
You'd say, 'Tusk! Tusk!'

Sally: A friend of mine fell from a window ten storeys up yesterday!
Tommy: Oh, I'm sorry to hear that. Was he hurt?
Sally: No — he fell inside!

What sort of lighting did Noah put in the ark?
Flood lighting.

What is a myth?
A lady with a lisp but no husband.

What sort of children does a florist have?
Budding geniuses or blooming idiots.

What do you get if you cross a cow with a mule?
Milk with a real kick in it.

What do you call pigs that live together?
Pen friends.

How do people eat cheese in Wales?
Caerphilly.

What did the python say to its victim?
I have a crush on you.

Gyles: What is everybody in the world doing at this very moment?
Arabella: I don't know — what are they doing?
Gyles: Growing older.

What is the difference between television and a newspaper?
You can't wrap fish and chips in a television.

Why did the sheep say 'Moo'?
She was learning a foreign language.

How do you pronounce VOLIX?
Volume nine.

What goes up in the air yellow and comes down
yellow and white?
An egg.

Who can shave three times a day but still have a
beard?
A barber.

Why did the fly fly?
Because the spider spied her.

How do you spell mousetrap in three letters?
C-A-T.

What did Vikings use for secret messages?
Norse Code.

How do they dance in Saudi Arabia?
Sheikh-to-Sheikh.

What was the largest island before Australia was

discovered?
Australia.

How do you keep cool at a football match?
Sit next to a fan.

How do you make a ham roll?
Push it.

Can a match box?
No, but a tin can.

What happened when the cat swallowed a penny?
There was money in the kitty.

What is the best way to hunt bear?
With your clothes off.

What is the wife of an engineer called?
Bridget.

Which is the house without a mouse?
A snail's house.

What has four legs and can fly?
Two birds.

What did the hamburger say to the tomato?
That is enough of your sauce!

Timmy: Did you hear the story about the shredded wheat and the corn flakes that had a fight?
Natasha: No, what happened?
Timmy: I can't tell you how it finished — it's a serial.

What do vegetarian cannibals eat?
Swedes.

What never asks questions but gets lots of answers?
A doorbell.

What was Yorick's nickname at school?
Numbskull.

What did the broken car horn say?

I don't give a hoot.

What do you do with a blue banana?
Try and cheer it up.

How do you keep flies out of the kitchen?
Put a bucket of manure in the lounge.

What do cannibals play at parties?
Swallow my leader.

What is the simplest and most effective method
of dieting?
Get lockjaw.

WAC BOOK LIST

For further reading you may be interested in the following, which are available from all good bookshops:

The Joys of Hitchhiking *Marsha Long*

The Greatest Detective Stories Ever *Wattes E. Dunn*

How I Won The Pools *Jack Potts*

How Not to Shoot Your Wife *Mr Completely*

Why You Need Insurance *Justin Case*

Don't Give Up *Percy Vere*

End of the Week *Gladys Friday*

All Aboard! *Abel Seamann*

Around the Mountain *Sheila B. Cumming*

The Pleasures of Horse-Riding *Jim Karna*

Outsize Clothes *L.E. Fant*

Neck Exercise *G. Rarff*

How to Diet *M.T. Cupboard*

Peek-a-Boo *I.C. Hugh*

How to Make an Igloo *S.K. Mow*

The Barber of Seville *Aaron Floor*

The Lost Bet *Henrietta Hatt*

The Flower Garden *Polly Anthus*

Hit On Head *I.C. Stars*

The World of Vegetables *Artie Choak*

Looking Forward *Felix Ited*

THANK YOU!

A special word of thanks to all WAC members who sent in the jokes for your very own Joke Book! We have not been able to thank everyone in person (partly because we could not read everybody's handwriting!) but here are the names of some of the people who sent in most jokes.

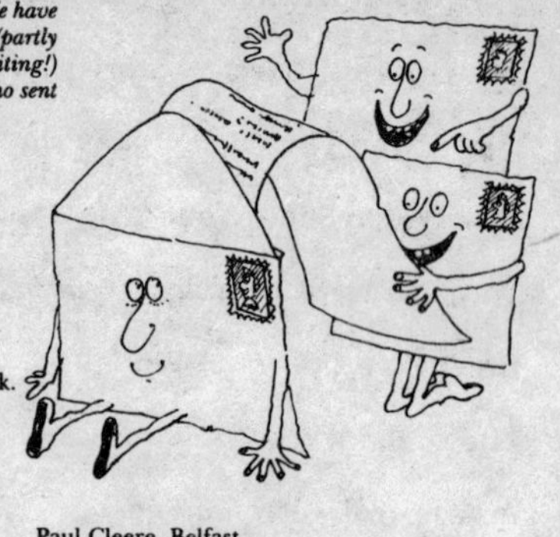

Margaret Gill, Huntingdon, Herts.
Samantha Sedley, Billericay, Essex.
James Collins, Swindon, Wilts.
Bill Notley, Glasgow.
Peter Wilkinson, Bury St Edmonds, Suffolk.
Martin Grafton, Bethnal Green, London.
Mary Smithson, Weston-super-Mare.
Raymond King, Clapham, London.
Monica Parkes, Bromley, Kent.
Alison Parton, Greenwich, London.
Paul Hammond, Dagenham, Essex.
Jo Little, Croydon, Surrey.
Roger Hall, Hammersmith, London.
Alan Knight, Torquay, Devon.
Colin Shaw, Jesmond, Tyne & Wear.
Paulette Cohen, Chinnor, Oxon.
Robert Jade, Liverpool.
Mick Melville, Stoke on Trent, Staffs.
Jay West, Weston, Avon.
Delia Cound, Wellington, Somerset.
Margaret Black, Stockton-on-Tees.
Sam Winter, Southampton.
Becky Whitworth, Isle of Wight.
Holly Bottomore, Catterick, N. Yorks.
Cliff Moore, Bristol.
Alex Cole, Ilford, Essex.
Meredith Border, Chichester, Sussex.
Craig Aveland, Coddington, Cheshire.
John Sumter, Henley-on-Thames.
Jenny Smith, Grasmere, Cumbria.
Jonathan Craig, Cambridge.
Mark Andrews, Maidenhead, Berks.
Mandy North, Thurlaston, Leicestershire.
Stan Gate, Throckley, Northumberland.
Lewis Barry, Holland Park, London.
Russell Cash, Boston, Lincs.
Mary Finch, Islington, London.
Libby Edwin, Huddersfield, W. Yorks.
Christopher Hall, The Barbican, London.
George Apostolides, Marylebone, London.
Tony Morris, Strathclyde.
Julie Belloch, Avington, Hants.
Anna Walters, Frampton, Dorset.
Elton Foulkes, Farnborough, Hants.
Andrew Wrathall, Wrexham, Clwyd.
Louise Nugent, Timperley, Cheshire.
Ebru Mustafa, Ponders End, Middlesex.
Natasha Girling, Camborne, Cornwall.
Iain Hutchins, Blackpool, Lancashire.
Neil Henderson, Linlithgow, West Lothian.
Tove-Lise Bakkan, Gosport, Hants.
Dawn Williams, Doncaster.
Clare Heider, Southampton.

Paul Cleere, Belfast.
Tim Kelley, Durham.
Karen Dagless, Peterborough, Cambs.
Danny Beckstead, Cardiff.
Yvette Polok, Market Harborough, Leics.
Russell Douglas, Heysham, Lancs.
Gareth Johns, Haverford West, Dyfed.
Mark Richardson, Bognor Regis, Sussex.
Paulette Redding, Hucknall, Notts.
Melanie Hudson, Coleraine, Northern Ireland.
Warren Bates, Flore, Northants.
Jennifer Haddell, Mickleover, Derby.
Paul Houston, Stroud, Glos.
Gemma Browne, Manchester.
Jamie Dacre, Cannock, Staffs.
Matthew Evanson, Gateshead, Tyne & Wear.
Susan Davidson, Rosyth, Fife.
Elinor Sefi, Thame, Oxon.
Sam Drewe, Greenock, Strathclyde.
Siobhan Glitherow, Richmond, Surrey.
Roger North, Johnby, Cumbria.
Ballal Gustasab, Birmingham.
Karen Thompson, Chester-le-Street, Durham.
Jeffrey Whiting, Ipswich, Suffolk.
Nick Bartree, Redruth, Cornwall.
Bernadette and Elizabeth Lynch, Glasgow.
Andrew Waites, Cookstown, Co. Tyrone.
Sue Pettey, Carlisle.
Glyn Jones, Anglesey.
Emily Alison, Basingstoke, Hants.
Brian Daniels, Shepperton, Middlesex.
David Sutherland, Iden, East Sussex.
Colin Morrison, Portsmouth, Hants.
Paul Hedger, Sawston, Cambs.
John Garrod, Skegness, Lincs.
Nick Poliakoff, Scunthorpe, Humber.
Miranda Bernstein, Harrogate, N. Yorks.
Rebecca Wetherby, Preston, Lancs.
Jackie Hutchings, Swansea.
Michelle Bennet, Stratford on Avon.
Grant Cumberland, Derrygonnelly, C. Fermanagh.
Robert McHenry, Lairg, Highlands.

Also available from Corgi Books:

WAC SNAX
A remarkable recipe book, stuffed full of hilarious and outrageous snacks devised by the Wide Awake Club viewers. In minutes you could create a delicious, mouthwatering and totally amazing WAC Snack!
0 552 54281 4

If you would like to receive a Newsletter about our new Children's books, just fill in the coupon below with your name and address (or copy it onto a separate piece of paper if you don't want to spoil your book) and send it to:

The Children's Books Editor
Young Corgi Books
61–63 Uxbridge Road
Ealing
London W5 5SA

Please send me a Children's Newsletter:

Name: ....

Address: ....

....

....

All Children's Books are available at your bookshop or news-agent, or can be ordered from the following address:
Corgi/Bantam Books,
Cash Sales Department,
P.O. Box 11, Falmouth, Cornwall TR10 9EN

Please send a cheque or postal order (no currency) and allow 60p for postage and packing for the first book plus 25p for the second book and 15p for each additional book ordered up to a maximum charge of £1.90 in UK.

B.F.P.O. customers please allow 60p for the first book, 25p for the second book plus 15p per copy for the next 7 books, thereafter 9p per book.

Overseas customers, including Eire, please allow £1.25 for postage and packing for the first book, 75p for the second book, and 28p for each subsequent title ordered.